Dr Jekyll and Mr Hyde

ROBERT LOUIS STEVENSON

Level 3

Retold by John Escott
Series Editors: Andy Hopkins and Jocelyn Potter

D1057046

Pearson Education Limited
Edinburgh Gate, Harlow,
Essex CM20 2JE, England
and Associated Companies throughout the world.

ISBN: 978-1-4058-5545-7

First published by Penguin Books 2000
This edition published 2008

9 10 8

Text copyright © Penguin Books Ltd 2000
This edition copyright © Pearson Education Ltd 2008
Illustrations by Tudor Humphries

Typeset by Graphicraft Ltd, Hong Kong
Set in 11/14pt Bembo
Printed in China
SWTC/08

Published by Pearson Education Ltd in association with
Penguin Books Ltd, both companies being subsidiaries of Pearson Plc

For a complete list of the titles available in the Penguin Readers series please write to your local
Pearson Longman office or to: Penguin Readers Marketing Department, Pearson Education,
Edinburgh Gate, Harlow, Essex CM20 2JE, England.

Contents

		page
Introduction		v
Chapter 1	The Door	1
Chapter 2	Mr Enfield's Story	2
Chapter 3	The Cheque	5
Chapter 4	Who is Mr Hyde?	6
Chapter 5	After Dinner	11
Chapter 6	The Carew Murder	12
Chapter 7	The Letter	17
Chapter 8	Dr Lanyon	21
Chapter 9	At the Window	25
Chapter 10	The Last Night	26
Chapter 11	Dr Lanyon's Story	34
Chapter 12	Henry Jekyll's Story	39
Chapter 13	The End of the Story	43
Activities		48

Introduction

Mr Hyde was pale and small, and he had an ugly smile. . . . But these were not important matters. They did not explain the feelings of hate and fear that Mr Utterson had. There was something more. The lawyer could not find a name for it.

'It is something about the man — some terrible evil,' he thought. 'Oh my poor Henry Jekyll! There is evil in the face of your new friend!'

Mr Utterson is worried about Dr Jekyll. Why has the doctor made a friend of the frightening Mr Hyde? Who *is* the evil little man? Where did he come from? And most important of all, why does he seem to have power over the good, honest Dr Jekyll?

Then comes the murder of Sir Davers Carew, and suddenly everybody in London is looking for Mr Hyde — the murderer. But the evil little man has disappeared.

Or has he?

As Mr Utterson tries to find answers to these questions, he learns the terrible secret of Dr Jekyll's dangerous experiments.

Robert Louis Stevenson was born in 1850 in Edinburgh, Scotland. He had no brothers or sisters and he was often ill as a child. So he was very lonely, but he loved writing. He spent a lot of time in bed, writing stories.

In 1867 he went to Edinburgh University, but he really wanted to be a writer. While he studied law at his parents' suggestion, he continued to write. At the age of twenty-five, he became a lawyer.

For the next four years Stevenson travelled, and in France he met Fanny Osbourne, an American woman. Fanny was married with two children and she was ten years older than Stevenson. She and Stevenson fell in love. Fanny left her husband, and in

1880 she and Stevenson were able to get married. The wedding was in the city of San Francisco, on the west coast of the United States.

But Stevenson was still not well. He spent most of his life trying to find a warm and comfortable place to live. He and Fanny spent years travelling, to Switzerland, Scotland, France, England and the United States. Then in 1890 they went to live on the Pacific island of Samoa. It was a very happy time for them. The people of Samoa called Stevenson 'the writer of stories'. But this happy time only lasted four years, and Stevenson died suddenly there in 1894, at the age of forty-four. Fanny died twenty years later.

Robert Louis Stevenson wrote many books. At first he wrote travel books and short stories. Many of these short stories were about the places he visited. *An Inland Voyage* (1878) is about a boat trip through Belgium and France. *Travels with a Donkey in the Cevennes* (1879) is about a walk through the mountains in southern France.

In 1882, Stevenson began to write longer books. *Treasure Island* is an exciting story about a young boy, Jim Hawkins. He goes on a journey to find gold. It is probably Stevenson's most famous book and children all over the world love it. Stevenson wrote it for Fanny Osbourne's young son, Lloyd. *Kidnapped* (1886), another adventure story, was also very successful. *Treasure Island* and *Kidnapped* are both Penguin Readers.

Stevenson wrote *The Strange Case of Dr Jekyll and Mr Hyde* in 1886 and it was very popular. It sold 40,000 copies in six months. The book made him famous in Britain and in the United States. 'The idea for the story came from a dream,' he told people. It is a mystery story, and the mystery is Mr Hyde. Who is he? What is he? The book is not a detective story. We are not trying to find out the name of the murderer. We know who the murderer is. It is Hyde.

In this book Stevenson writes about the two sides of people – the good and the bad sides – and about right and wrong. *Dr Jekyll and Mr Hyde* asks interesting questions about people and their actions which are still important today.

There have been many films and plays of *Dr Jekyll and Mr Hyde*. There have also been many other books, films and plays about good and evil in people. Think about Darth Vader and Anakin Skywalker in *Star Wars*, for example. More than a hundred and thirty years after it was written, Robert Louis Stevenson's *Dr Jekyll and Mr Hyde* is still a very popular story.

Chapter 1   The Door

Mr John Utterson was a lawyer and he lived in London. He seemed to be a cold man, without feeling. He never smiled, and he spoke only when it was necessary. But people liked him. There was something in his eyes that showed kindness. It showed his understanding of other people. Men and women came to him about the law, and he helped them all. It did not matter who they were.

He lived a quiet and simple life. He enjoyed the theatre, but he did not visit it any more. His friends were people from his family, and very old friends from his old school.

Then there was Mr Enfield. Other people could see no reason for Mr Utterson and Mr Richard Enfield to be friends. Mr Enfield was quite different from Mr Utterson. He was younger, and enjoyed going to the theatre, to parties and good restaurants.

'Why are they friends?' people asked. 'What do they talk about when they are together?'

And the reply was: 'If you see them on their Sunday walks, they never say anything. They don't seem to enjoy themselves.'

But the two men thought that their Sunday walks were an important part of the week. They enjoyed being together, and they enjoyed the walks. But they were often silent walks.

On one of their walks the two men found themselves in a narrow street in one of the busier parts of London. It was a quiet street on a Sunday, but during the week the little shops on each side were very busy. Because the shops were successful, they were clean and brightly painted. The road was clean. It was a pleasant street to walk along.

Near one end of this street, there was a break in the line of shops. There was a narrow entrance to a courtyard, and next to it was the windowless end of a tall, dark, ugly house. A door in this wall was unpainted and needed repair. Old men sometimes slept in the doorway, and small boys sometimes played on the steps and wrote their names on the door with their pocket knives.

Mr Enfield and the lawyer were on the other side of the street, but Mr Enfield pointed to it with his walking stick.

'Have you ever noticed that door before, John?' he asked.

'Yes. Ugly, isn't it?' replied Mr Utterson.

'Every time I pass it,' said Mr Enfield, 'I think about a day last winter. A very strange thing happened.'

'Oh?' said Mr Utterson. 'What was it?'

Chapter 2   Mr Enfield's Story

'One dark morning, I was on my way home at about three o'clock. At first I walked a very long way without seeing anyone. Everybody was asleep. The street lights were lit, but the street was empty and silent.

'Suddenly I saw two people. One was a little man who was walking quickly towards the street corner. The other was a little girl. She was about eight or nine years old, I think. She was running as quickly as she could towards the same corner. Naturally, she ran into the little man.

'And then I saw something terrible. The girl fell down, and the man calmly *walked on her*. He stepped on her body! She cried out, of course, but he did not stop or turn round – he just walked away! He wasn't acting like a man – more like a mindless machine. Then the girl started screaming.

'I shouted and ran after the man. At last I caught him by the neck, and brought him back. Already there was a group of people round the crying child – her family, and some of her neighbours.

' "Get a doctor!" said somebody, and one of the neighbours hurried away.

'Have you ever noticed that door before, John?'

'He was quite calm – the man who stepped on the child. He did not try to escape. But he looked at me once, and my blood ran cold. I hated him.

'The people round the girl were soon joined by the doctor. The girl was not hurt very much – only frightened really, the doctor said. But there was something very unusual about it all. I felt an immediate hate for the man that I was holding. The child's family hated him too, and that was natural. But the doctor was not like us. He was the usual cold, calm scientific man. But every time he looked at the man, I saw him turn sick and white.

' "He wants to kill him, too," I thought.

'I understood what was in the doctor's mind. He looked at me. He knew what was in mine.

' "We can't kill the man, even if we want to," we agreed. But we promised to make as much trouble for him as we could.

' "We'll tell all our friends about this!" we told the man. "Everyone in London will hear about it!"

'And all the time, we were keeping the women away from him. They were wild and dangerous because they were so angry. I never saw so many hate-filled faces. And there was the man, in the middle. He was frightened, but he smiled an ugly smile and did not move.

' "If you want money," he said, "tell me. Nobody wants trouble with people like you."

'We told him to give a hundred pounds to the child and her family. At first he didn't want to agree to this, but the little crowd round him looked dangerous, and at last he said, "All right, I'll pay."

'Next, we had to get the money. And where do you think he took us? To that ugly place with the door! He pulled a key out of his pocket, unlocked the door and went in.

'We waited outside. After a time, he came out with ten pounds in money, and a cheque for the rest. The cheque was signed, and the signature surprised me. It was the name of a famous man! I can't tell you the name, but you probably know it well.

'"I don't like this," I said. "You walk through a door like that at four o'clock in the morning, and come out of it with another man's cheque for nearly a hundred pounds! It's very unusual."

'He smiled his ugly smile again and answered, "You don't need to worry. I'll stay with you until the banks open. And then I'll get the money with the cheque."

'The child's father, the man and I went to my house and waited there until the morning. After breakfast, we all went to the bank together, with the cheque. And the bank paid the money without question.'

Chapter 3   The Cheque

Mr Utterson looked shocked. 'Oh, dear!' he said. 'That's a terrible story!'

'Yes, I agree,' said Mr Enfield. 'It's a shocking story. Nobody would like the unpleasant man who hurt the girl. But another man signed the cheque, and he is exactly the opposite. A really fine, honest man, and very famous for his good work.'

'What is the name of the man who walked over the child?' asked Mr Utterson.

'His name is Mr Hyde,' said Mr Enfield.

'And the man who signed the cheque? Does he live in that house?' asked Mr Utterson. 'Do you know?'

'Behind that door?' Mr Enfield said. 'No, he doesn't. His house is in a square, but I don't remember the name of the square. The place behind the door doesn't really seem like a house. There are three windows on the first floor over the courtyard. They are always shut, but they are clean. Somebody lives there. But the houses are all near together round the courtyard. You can't be sure how many there are. There doesn't seem to be another door. And nobody uses the door that I showed you. Except the man that I have told you about.'

Mr Utterson walked in silence. It was clear that he was thinking. At last he said, 'Are you sure that he used a key?'

Mr Enfield was clearly surprised. 'Well . . .' he began.

The lawyer continued, 'I'm sorry. It must seem a strange question, but there is a reason for it. I already know the name of the man who signed the cheque.'

Chapter 4   Who is Mr Hyde?

That evening, Mr Utterson ate his dinner without much interest. He was not really hungry. There was too much on his mind. After dinner he usually read a book until midnight, and then went to bed.

But that night he took a light and went into his office. There he opened his safe and took out an envelope. On it were the words: 'Dr Jekyll's Will'. He sat down and began to read the will with a worried look on his face.

The will was in Dr Jekyll's writing. Mr Utterson refused to help the doctor when he wrote it. The lawyer had to keep it for the doctor – it was his job – but he did not like the will.

The will was clear. 'If Henry Jekyll dies, his house and all his money passes into the hands of his friend and helper, Edward Hyde.' And 'if Dr Jekyll disappears for three months, the same Edward Hyde will own everything immediately.'

The lawyer disliked this will. He did not like it as a lawyer, and it made him angry as a person. He liked people to do things in an ordinary way.

'My dislike was very strong when Hyde was only a name,' he said to himself. 'Now I know some very unpleasant things about the man with that name, and it makes it worse. I thought that Jekyll was mad. Now I'm beginning to think he's afraid.'

After some time, he put the will back into his safe, then he put on a coat and hat and went out into the cold night. He went to Cavendish Square to visit his friend, the famous Dr Lanyon.

'If someone knows something about this, it is Lanyon,' he thought.

He soon reached Cavendish Square and his friend's house. Dr Lanyon's servant was glad to see Mr Utterson, and took the lawyer straight to the dining-room. Dr Lanyon was finishing his dinner. The doctor was a happy, healthy man with a red face. When he saw Mr Utterson, he jumped up.

'It's good to see you, Utterson,' he said. 'Sit down and make yourself comfortable.'

They always enjoyed their visits. After a little general talk, the lawyer spoke about Dr Jekyll.

'You and I, Lanyon, are surely Henry Jekyll's two oldest friends,' he said.

'It is a pity that the friends are not younger,' said Dr Lanyon, smiling. 'But, yes, we probably are his oldest friends. But I don't see him very often now.'

'Oh? Is that right? I'm surprised to hear it,' said Mr Utterson. 'I thought that you were both interested in the same scientific work.'

'We were,' Dr Lanyon replied. 'But then Henry Jekyll began to have some strange ideas. Ideas that I could not agree with. He began to go wrong, or that is my opinion. How? Wrong in the mind, I think. Of course, I am still interested in him.'

Utterson waited for a minute, then asked, 'Did you ever meet a man that he knows – a man with the name of Hyde?'

'Hyde?' said Lanyon quickly. 'No. I never heard Henry Jekyll say that name.'

And that was all the information that Mr Utterson went home with that evening. But Enfield's story did not leave his mind. He could not stop thinking about it, and he slept badly that night.

'I must see this Mr Hyde,' he thought. 'I must see this man that Enfield hates so strongly. The man seems to have power over Henry Jekyll. Perhaps then I shall understand the mystery of Dr Jekyll's will.'

◆

From that day, Mr Utterson began to watch the door in the street of little shops when he had time. He watched it in the morning before he went to his office. He watched at lunchtime when the street was busy. He watched again at night under the moonlight. He was a patient man.

And at last, at about ten o'clock one cold night, he heard some quick steps coming towards the door.

Mr Utterson stepped into the entrance to the courtyard.

The man walked quickly round the corner. He was small, and was dressed in very plain clothes. Utterson could not see the man's face clearly, but he still felt a strong dislike for him.

The man walked straight towards the door, and took a key from his pocket.

Mr Utterson moved out and touched him on the shoulder. 'Mr Hyde, I think?' he said.

Mr Hyde moved a step away. But if he was afraid, his fear quickly disappeared. He did not look at the lawyer's face, but he said quite coldly: 'That is my name. What do you want?'

'I see that you are going in,' the lawyer answered. 'I am an old friend of Dr Jekyll's. I am sure that you have heard my name – Mr Utterson of Gaunt Street. Perhaps you'll save my tired feet and give me your permission to go in with you through this door.'

'You won't find Dr Jekyll at home,' replied Mr Hyde. 'He is out.' And then suddenly, but still without looking up, he said, 'How did you know me?'

'Before I answer your question, will you do something for me?' said Utterson.

'Of course,' said the other man.

'Can I see your face?' said Utterson.

Mr Hyde seemed to think for a minute. Then he turned round and looked straight at Mr Utterson.

'Thank you,' said Utterson. 'Now I will know you again.'

'Yes,' said Hyde. 'And you can have my address, too.' And he gave Utterson a card with an address in Soho.

Mr Utterson was surprised. 'Why did he give me his address?' he thought. 'Is he thinking of Henry Jekyll's will?' He did not show what he was feeling. He put the card in his pocket and said, 'Thank you.'

'And now I will repeat my question,' said Hyde. 'How did you know me?'

'By description.'

'Who described me?' said Hyde.

Mr Utterson thought quickly. 'There are people who know both of us,' he said.

'Who are they?'

'Jekyll is one,' said the lawyer.

'He did not tell you about me!' cried Mr Hyde angrily. 'Don't lie!' And moving quickly, he went to the door. He unlocked it, and disappeared into the house.

Mr Utterson stood for a minute. Then he walked slowly away, turning a problem over in his mind. Mr Hyde was pale and small, and he had an ugly smile. He spoke to the lawyer in a soft, broken voice, mixing politeness and rudeness. But these were not important matters. They did not explain the feelings of hate and fear that Mr Utterson had. There was something more. The lawyer could not find a name for it.

'It is something about the man – some terrible evil,' he thought. 'Oh, my poor Henry Jekyll! There is evil in the face of your new friend!'

◆

Around the corner at the end of the street of small shops there was a square of old houses. They were nearly all flats and offices now, but one house, the second from the corner, was still owned by one person. Mr Utterson went to the door of this house and knocked.

A well-dressed old servant opened the door.

'Is Dr Jekyll at home, Poole?' asked the lawyer.

'I will go and see, Mr Utterson,' said Poole. 'Come in.'

He showed the lawyer into a large room and pointed to a big chair.

'Would you like to sit there, sir?' said Poole. 'I won't be long.'

'Thank you,' said Mr Utterson.

He liked waiting in this room. He usually thought how pleasant it was. But tonight he could not forget the face of Mr Hyde. It seemed to be in every corner of the room, in every moving light that burned in the fireplace.

Mr Utterson was worried and afraid. He sat and thought. He did not know what to say to his friend.

Then Poole came back. Mr Utterson was really quite glad when he said, 'Dr Jekyll has gone out, sir.'

'I saw Mr Hyde go in by the old workroom door, Poole,' he said. 'Is that all right, when Dr Jekyll is out?'

'Yes, it is usual, sir,' the servant replied.

'Are you sure?' said Utterson.

'Yes,' said Poole. 'Mr Hyde has a key.'

'Does he?' said Utterson. 'Dr Jekyll seems to trust that young man, Poole.'

'Yes, sir, he does,' said Poole. 'Dr Jekyll has told us to take orders from Mr Hyde. When he is not here, Mr Hyde takes his place.'

'I don't think I have ever met Mr Hyde here,' said Mr Utterson.

'Oh, no, sir. He never comes to dinner here,' replied the servant. 'In fact, we don't often see him in this house. He usually comes and goes through the workroom.'

They were silent for a minute or two, then Mr Utterson said, 'Good night, Poole.'

'Good night, Mr Utterson,' said Poole.

The lawyer started to walk home. He was very sad as he thought about his friend.

'Poor Henry Jekyll,' he thought. 'I am afraid that he is in some sort of trouble. He was quite wild when he was a young man.

Has something come back from the past to destroy him now? I hope not.'

So Hyde was free to come and go in Jekyll's house. That worried Utterson. 'If that evil man learns about the will,' he thought, 'perhaps he will want to hurry Jekyll's death. Or help him to disappear. Then he will be able to enjoy the things that Jekyll owns now. I must do something about it, if Jekyll will let me. *If* he will let me.'

Chapter 5   After Dinner

Mr Utterson was very glad when, about two weeks later, Dr Jekyll gave one of his pleasant dinner parties for five or six old friends. They were all intelligent men, and they all enjoyed good conversation and fine wine, so they were happy to come to the doctor's house. And as usual, the lawyer stayed after the others went home.

Mr Utterson and Dr Jekyll sat together, one on each side of the fireplace.

'I wanted to speak to you, Jekyll,' Utterson began.

'Oh?' said the doctor. 'What about?'

'About your will,' said the lawyer.

It was clear that the doctor did not like the subject. But he smiled. 'My poor Utterson,' he said. 'I am very sorry that it worries you. You worry more than anyone. Oh, except Lanyon – he seems worried about my scientific work. But he is a good man, like you.'

'You know that I never liked that will,' said the lawyer. He refused to talk about other things.

'Yes, I know that,' said the doctor. 'You told me.'

'Well, I'll tell you again,' said Utterson. 'And I have learned something about Hyde.'

Dr Jekyll's face went pale. 'I don't want to listen,' he said.

'I heard a very bad thing,' said Utterson.

'It doesn't change anything,' said Jekyll.

'It must,' said Utterson.

'I am sorry, but you don't understand, Utterson,' said the doctor. 'It is a very strange business – very strange. It won't become better if we talk about it. There is nothing more to say about it.'

'Henry,' said Utterson, 'you know me. You know that you can trust me. Tell me all about it. I am sure that I can get you out of trouble.'

'You are a really good man, Utterson,' the doctor said. 'I can't find words to thank you. I trust you more than any other person. But it isn't what you think. I can tell you one thing. When I want to, I can be free of Hyde.'

Mr Utterson started to speak, but Jekyll stopped him.

'You should know something,' said Jekyll. 'I am very interested in poor Hyde. I know that you have seen him. He told me that. And I am afraid that he was not polite. But I do take great interest in that young man. I want to ask you to do what is right. Help him to get the things that are in my will. Can you give me that promise? It is very important to me.'

'I can't say that I will ever like him,' said the lawyer.

'I don't ask for that,' said Jekyll. He put his hand on his old friend's arm. 'You are my friend. I only want you to help him when I die.'

Utterson looked very unhappy. But at last he said, 'All right. I promise.'

Chapter 6   The Carew Murder

Nearly a year later, in October 1880, there was a terrible crime in a London street. Everyone in London was shocked when they heard about it.

There was a terrible crime in a London street.

A young woman servant saw it happen. She lived alone in a house not far from the river. At about eleven o'clock on the night of the crime, she went up to her room. She sat on a chair near the window and looked out at the moonlit streets. She was a romantic young woman and she began to think about love.

After a time, she noticed an old man with white hair coming along the narrow street below her window. Then she saw another, very small man going along the street the opposite way. This man carried a heavy stick in his hand. When the two men were quite close, the old man stopped. He seemed to ask the small man a polite question. The girl saw him pointing. She thought that he was asking the way. The moon shone on the old man's kind face as he spoke.

The girl looked at the other man. To her surprise, she knew his face. He was a man, Mr Hyde, who once visited her employer. She remembered feeling a strong dislike for him at that time.

Suddenly this Mr Hyde became crazy with anger! He waved his stick and started shouting. The old man looked very surprised. He took a step back. And then Mr Hyde really went mad ('like a wild animal', as the girl described it later).

He hit the old man over the head with his stick, and knocked him to the ground. Then he jumped on the old man's body and hit him again and again with the heavy stick. He did not stop until the old man was dead.

This terrible thing was too much for the girl. She fell to the floor, her eyes closed, and for some time she knew nothing.

It was two o'clock before the girl opened her eyes again. When she remembered the murder, she immediately called the police.

The murderer was not there, of course, but the murdered man was still on the ground in the middle of the narrow street. The heavy stick was broken, and one half of it lay near the body.

The police looked in the murdered man's pockets and found some money and a gold watch. There was also a letter, ready to post. The envelope had Mr Utterson's name and address on it.

A police inspector brought this letter to the lawyer just before nine o'clock in the morning. He told Mr Utterson about the crime.

Mr Utterson listened carefully, then he said, 'This is a very serious matter. But I don't want to say anything until I see the body.'

'I'll take you now,' said the police inspector.

The body was at the police station. When Utterson saw it, he said, 'Yes, I know him. This is the body of Sir Danvers Carew.'

'Really, sir?' said the police inspector. 'He's a very famous man.'

And Utterson could see the police inspector thinking, 'Yes, and perhaps I'll be famous, too, if I catch the murderer!'

'Yes,' said Utterson. 'Sir Danvers was very famous.'

'Perhaps you will be able to help us in our search for the killer, sir,' the police inspector said. He told Utterson what the girl saw.

Mr Utterson was worried when he heard the name of Hyde. Then he saw the broken stick – and he knew it immediately.

'I gave it to Henry Jekyll personally, many years ago,' he thought. But he said nothing.

The police inspector was waiting for Mr Utterson to say something, so the lawyer asked, 'Is this Mr Hyde a small man?'

'Yes,' said the police inspector. 'Very small, and very evil-looking, the servant-girl says.'

Mr Utterson thought for a moment. Then he said: 'Come with me. I think that I can take you to his house.'

◆

The taxi moved slowly through the streets with Mr Utterson and the police inspector in the back. The address on Hyde's card was not a pleasant part of Soho. The street was narrow and dirty. Between the houses, there was a cheap French eating house and some small shops. Poor children in dirty clothes sat in doorways.

The taxi stopped outside Hyde's house, and Utterson and the police inspector got out. Mr Utterson knocked on the door. An old woman opened it. She had silver-coloured hair and an unpleasant face, but she spoke politely and answered Mr Utterson's question.

'Yes,' she said. 'This is Mr Hyde's house, but Mr Hyde is not at home.' And in answer to more questions from Mr Utterson she said, 'Yes, Mr Hyde came in very late last night. That's not unusual. He comes and goes at all sorts of times, and he's often away.'

'When did you last see him before last night?' asked Utterson.

'More than two months ago,' said the woman. 'He went out one day and I didn't see him again.'

'We want to see his rooms,' said Utterson.

'That's impossible –' the woman began.

Utterson stopped her. 'This person is Police Inspector Newcome,' he said.

An unpleasant smile came to the woman's face. 'Ah!' she said. 'Mr Hyde is in trouble! What did he do?'

The inspector did not answer. 'Just show us his rooms,' he said.

The rooms had good furniture, and some good pictures on the wall. But there were signs that the place was left in a hurry. There were clothes lying on the floor, but with nothing in the pockets. There were a lot of burned papers in the fireplace. From some of the half-burned papers, the inspector pulled out part of a cheque book. Then he found the other end of the broken stick behind the door.

'Now we've got him,' the police inspector said to Mr Utterson. 'We must just wait for him at the bank. He can't do anything without money.'

But it was not as easy as that. Police watched the bank, but Mr Hyde did not go near it. It wasn't possible to get a good description of the man, and there were no photographs of him. People gave very different descriptions of him, but they all agreed about one thing. He looked wild and evil, and there was something terrible about him.

16

Chapter 7   The Letter

It was late in the afternoon when Mr Utterson went to Dr Jekyll's house. Poole opened the door to him, and the lawyer and the servant crossed the courtyard behind the house and went into the workroom.

The workroom was for Dr Jekyll's scientific experiments. Above it there was a large room where the doctor had his desk, hundreds of books and things for his experiments. On one wall of this room was a large mirror. There was a fire in the fireplace. Near it, Dr Jekyll was sitting silently. He looked very ill.

After Poole left them, Mr Utterson said, 'Have you heard the news?'

'Yes, I have heard,' the doctor said. His face was white. 'The newspaper boys were shouting it outside in the streets. I heard them from my dining-room.'

'Then tell me one thing, Jekyll,' said the lawyer. 'Sir Danvers Carew was my client, but you are too. I want to know what I am doing. You aren't mad enough to hide this man Hyde, are you?'

'No, Utterson,' said the doctor. 'I promise that I will never see him again. It is all finished. I'll never have any more business with him. He is safe, and nobody will ever hear of him again.'

The lawyer was very worried about his friend. Dr Jekyll seemed very ill.

'You seem very sure, Henry,' Utterson said. 'I hope that you are right. Please understand – if they catch the man, people will talk about you too.'

'I am sure,' Jekyll answered. 'I have a good reason to be sure, but I cannot explain it. But you can help me with one thing. I . . . I had a letter. I am not sure that I should show it to the police. You can decide, Utterson. I know I can trust you.'

'You are afraid that it will help the police,' said Mr Utterson. 'Is that right?'

17

Dr Jekyll was sitting silently. He looked very ill.

'No,' said the doctor. 'I'm not worried about Hyde, or what happens to him. I have finished with him – completely finished. I was thinking of my good name.'

'Show me the letter,' said the lawyer.

The letter was written in unusual handwriting:

Dear Dr Jekyll,

    You have helped me in a thousand ways. I am afraid that I have paid you for your kindness with some very bad actions. But you do not need to worry about me. I will be safe because I have a sure way to escape.

    Please forgive and forget me.

                    Edward Hyde.

Mr Utterson liked the letter. It showed that he could worry a little less.

'Do you have the envelope?' he asked.

'I burned it without thinking,' Jekyll answered. 'But the letter was not posted, I know that. Somebody brought it to the house.'

Mr Utterson thought for a minute. Then he said, 'If you agree, I'll keep the letter until tomorrow. I'll think about it.'

'Please do that,' said Jekyll.

'And now, I have one more question,' said Mr Utterson. 'Was it Hyde who wanted you to put that sentence in your will? The sentence about your disappearance?'

'Yes,' said the doctor, quietly.

'I knew it,' said Utterson. 'He wanted to murder you. You have had a lucky escape.'

'I have had something much more important,' the doctor said seriously. 'I have had a lesson. Oh, Utterson, I have learned a lesson!'

On his way out, the lawyer stopped and spoke to Poole. 'Somebody brought a letter for the doctor this morning, Poole,' he said. 'Can you describe the person who brought it to the door?'

'No letters came today,' the old servant said. 'Only a few that the postman brought – all bills.'

Mr Utterson's fears were as great as before when he walked home. 'It seems that the letter came through the workroom door,' he thought. 'Or perhaps it was written in the workroom! If that is true, I must be very careful.'

The newspaper boys were shouting in the streets of the city.

'Read all about it! Sir Danvers Carew murdered! Read all about it!'

◆

A few hours later, Mr Utterson was sitting by the fire in his own office. With him was his head clerk, Mr Guest. Utterson trusted his clerk. Guest often went to Dr Jekyll's house on business for Mr Utterson, and he knew Poole.

'Perhaps he also knows about Mr Hyde's visits to the house,' thought Utterson.

Mr Utterson decided to show Guest the letter which explained some of the mystery. There was another good reason for showing Guest the letter. Guest was very clever about handwriting.

'This is terrible news about Sir Danvers Carew,' Mr Utterson said.

'Yes, sir, terrible,' said Guest. 'The murderer was mad, of course.'

'I'd like to hear what you think about that,' the lawyer said. 'I have a letter here in his handwriting. Will you look at it?'

Guest looked surprised, but said nothing.

'Perhaps you are interested to see a murderer's handwriting,' Mr Utterson continued. 'I am not sure what to do about the letter. It must be a secret between the two of us. But I would like to hear your opinion about the handwriting.'

Guest studied the letter with great interest.

'No, sir,' he said at last. 'Not mad. But it is very strange handwriting.'

Just then, a servant came in with a note for Mr Utterson.

'Is that from Dr Jekyll, sir?' the clerk asked.

'Yes,' said Utterson.

'I thought that I knew the writing,' said Guest. 'Is it private, Mr Utterson?'

'No, it is only a dinner invitation,' said Utterson. 'Why? Do you want to see it?'

'Just for a minute, sir, please.' And the clerk put the two pieces of paper side by side and studied them with great interest.

'Thank you, sir,' he said at last, and he gave both the notes back to Mr Utterson.

There was a minute of silence. Then the lawyer asked the question that Guest was waiting for. Mr Utterson was afraid that he already knew the answer.

'Why did you look at the two together, Guest?' asked Utterson.

'Well, sir, in very many ways the handwriting is the same,' said Guest.

'That's strange,' said Utterson.

'Yes,' Guest agreed. 'Very strange.'

'But it isn't information to tell other people,' said the lawyer carefully.

'No, sir,' said the clerk. 'I understand.' And he turned and left the room.

When Mr Utterson was alone, he locked the note in his safe. 'I don't understand it,' he thought. 'Henry Jekyll wrote a letter for a murderer!'

And the blood ran cold through his body.

Chapter 8   Dr Lanyon

Time passed. Thousands of pounds were offered for information about Sir Danvers Carew's murderer. Where was Mr Hyde?

Nobody knew. The police heard a lot about him. They heard stories about his crimes. They heard about the hate that people felt for him. But where was he? After he left the house in Soho on that morning of the murder, nobody heard of Mr Hyde again.

Mr Utterson slowly stopped being worried, and his friend Dr Jekyll was enjoying a new life now without Mr Hyde. The doctor visited his old friends again, and there were dinners, drinking and pleasant talk, like the old days.

On the eighth of January, Utterson had dinner at Jekyll's house with a small number of other guests. Dr Lanyon was there, and the three of them were soon talking like old friends again. It was very pleasant.

Then, on the twelfth of January, and again on the fourteenth, Utterson tried to see his friend, but without any success. Each time, Poole answered the door.

'The doctor is not able to leave the house, sir,' said the servant. 'He will not see any visitors.'

On the fifteenth of January Mr Utterson tried again, with the same result. He was worried and unhappy. What was wrong with his friend?

At last he went to see Dr Lanyon. He thought that the doctor's servant looked worried. But the man took him in immediately to Lanyon.

Mr Utterson was shocked at the change in his friend. The usually healthy-looking man was pale and sick. He looked much older and thinner. The lawyer was sure that Lanyon was dying. But the look in the doctor's eyes was worse than this. It was a look of terrible fear, of something in the mind that was killing him.

'You don't look well,' said the lawyer. 'Is it something serious, old friend?'

'I had a shock,' said Dr Lanyon. And then he continued, 'I won't get better. I have only a few weeks to live. Life has been pleasant – I have enjoyed it. But if we know everything, we are happier to leave this life.'

'Jekyll is ill, too,' said Utterson. 'Have you seen him?'

Lanyon held up a hand that was shaking with weakness – or strong feelings. 'I don't want to see Dr Jekyll again or to hear anything about him,' he said.

'That is very sad,' Utterson said. 'Can I do anything to help? We have been three very good friends, Lanyon. We are too old to make new friends now.'

'No,' said Lanyon. 'You can't do anything, Utterson. Ask Jekyll.'

'He won't see me,' said the lawyer. 'I've tried. He won't give me permission to go into his house.'

'I am not surprised,' was the reply. 'One day soon, Utterson, after I am dead, you will perhaps learn the true story.'

'Can't you tell me now?' asked Utterson.

'No, I can't tell you,' said Lanyon. 'Now, if you can talk to me about other things, that will be good. But if you can't keep away from that subject, please go.'

After he got home, Utterson sat down and wrote a letter to Jekyll. He wrote:

> I am sorry that you will not see me. And what happened between you and Lanyon?

An answer came the next day. It was a long and strange reply. Towards the end, Utterson read:

> I agree with Lanyon – we must never meet again. I cannot tell you the reason. In future I am going to see very few people. My door is shut to you. But you must be sure that I am still your friend.
>
> I have brought to myself a danger that I cannot tell you about. My suffering and fears are worse than I can describe. There is only one thing that you can do to help me, Utterson. Leave me alone.
>
> Henry Jekyll

Mr Utterson could not understand the sudden change. Until a week ago, the doctor seemed happy with life again. What went wrong? Was Jekyll mad? The lawyer remembered Lanyon's words. He knew that there was no simple reason.

◆

A week later, Dr Lanyon was in bed, and two weeks after that, he died. Mr Utterson was very sad about the death of his old friend as he sat down in Lanyon's office. He opened an envelope. On it were the words:

Private. For the eyes of J. G. Utterson only.

That was in Dr Lanyon's handwriting. Inside the envelope there was another envelope. On it were more words in Dr Lanyon's writing:

Do not open until Dr Henry Jekyll dies or disappears.

Mr Utterson could not believe his eyes. Here was the word again! *Disappears*! Here again, like in Jekyll's will, was the idea that the doctor could disappear. The idea came from the evil man Hyde, but here it was in Dr Lanyon's handwriting. Utterson wanted to open the envelope and read, but he was a good and honest lawyer. He locked it in the back of his safe, unopened.

◆

He went quite often to Dr Jekyll's house, but he did not see the doctor. Poole came to the door, but had no good news for him.

'The doctor spends nearly all his time in the room above the workroom,' said Poole. 'Sometimes he even sleeps there. He is strangely silent, Mr Utterson, and his servants are all worried about him.'

'Thank you for telling me, Poole,' said Mr Utterson.

Chapter 9   At the Window

One Sunday, on their usual walk, Mr Utterson and Mr Enfield found themselves in the narrow street where Dr Jekyll's workroom door was.

They stopped and looked at the door.

'Well, that story's finished,' said Enfield. 'We won't see Mr Hyde again.'

'I hope not,' said Utterson. 'Did I ever tell you that I once saw him? And I had the same feelings of fear and hate that you described.'

'Everybody seemed to have the same feelings,' Enfield replied. 'But at the time of my story, I didn't know that this was a back way to Dr Jekyll's house. It was silly of me.'

'Well, let's step into the courtyard and look at the windows,' said Utterson. 'I am worried about poor Jekyll. Even if we can't go in, he will be able to hear a friend's voice.'

'That's true,' said Enfield.

The sun was high in the sky, but it was cold in the courtyard, and a little dark. The middle one of the three windows was half open. Utterson saw Jekyll sitting close to it. He looked very sad, like an unhappy prisoner.

'Hello!' called Utterson, 'Hello, Jekyll! I hope that you are feeling better.'

'I am not well, Utterson,' the doctor answered weakly. 'I am very ill.'

'You stay inside too much,' the lawyer said. 'You should be outside, walking like Enfield and me. Get your hat and come for a quick walk with us. You will feel much better.'

The doctor came nearer to the window. 'You are very good,' he said. 'It is kind of you to ask me. I would like that very much. But . . . no . . . no, it is not possible. I can't go with you.'

'Are you sure?' said Utterson.

'I am sure,' replied the doctor. 'But I am very glad to see you, Utterson. I would like to ask you and Mr Enfield to come up, but the place is not tidy.'

'Then we can stay down here,' Utterson said, 'and talk to you.'

Dr Jekyll smiled. 'That is a kind suggestion,' he said. But suddenly the smile disappeared from his face and a look of terrible fear took its place. The two men below felt their blood freeze.

They saw it only for a second or two, because Jekyll shut the window immediately. But it was enough. They both turned silently and left the courtyard.

When they reached a busy street again, Mr Utterson at last looked at his friend. Both of their faces were pale, and there was a shocked look in their eyes.

'God forgive us!' said Mr Utterson.

The two men walked again in silence.

Chapter 10   The Last Night

Mr Utterson was sitting alone one evening after dinner when Poole arrived at his house. The lawyer was surprised to see him.

'Hello, Poole,' he said. 'What is this visit about?' And then when he looked again at Dr Jekyll's servant, he continued, 'What's the matter? Is the doctor ill?'

'Mr Utterson,' Poole said. 'Something is terribly wrong.'

'Sit down and tell me about it,' said the lawyer.

'Thank you, sir,' said Poole.

'Where is the doctor?' asked Utterson.

'Well, sir, that's the trouble,' said Poole. 'You know that he shuts himself in the room above the workroom. But something's wrong – terribly wrong. I'm afraid, Mr Utterson. I've been afraid for a week now. I had to come and see you tonight.'

Utterson said, 'What do you mean? What are you afraid of, Poole?'

'I can't say, sir,' said Poole. 'But will you come with me – please, sir – please – and see with your own eyes?'

Mr Utterson's only answer was to get his hat and coat. Then the two men left the house.

It was a wild, cold night in March and there were no people in the streets. The two men walked quickly, and in silence.

When they reached Dr Jekyll's front door, Poole knocked in a special way, and a voice from inside asked, 'Is that you, Mr Poole?'

'It's all right,' answered Poole. 'You can open the door. It's me – Poole.'

The door opened, and all Dr Jekyll's servants were waiting inside. When they saw Mr Utterson, one cried, 'Thank God! It's Mr Utterson!'

'Why are you all here?' Utterson wanted to know.

'They're all afraid,' said Poole. 'Will you come with me, sir? Come as quietly as you can, Mr Utterson. I want you to hear, but I don't want him to hear you.'

And he walked out to the courtyard at the back of the house. Utterson followed him.

'One other thing, sir,' Poole said. 'If he asks you to go in, don't go, sir, please.'

They went through the workroom to the bottom of the stairs. Here Poole spoke quietly to Mr Utterson.

'Stand on one side and listen,' he said.

Then he went up the stairs and knocked on the door of the room above.

'Mr Utterson is asking to see you, sir!' Poole called.

An angry voice came from the other side of the door: 'I can't see anyone.'

'Thank you, sir,' said Poole.

He took Mr Utterson back to the house.

'Sir,' he said, looking into the lawyer's eyes, 'was that the doctor's voice?'

'It seems to be greatly changed,' Utterson replied.

'Changed?' said Poole. 'I have been here in Dr Jekyll's house for twenty years, and I know his voice. That isn't it. No, sir. The doctor is dead. He was killed a week ago, when we heard him cry to God. But who is in there now, Mr Utterson? And why does he stay there? That's what I want to know!'

'This is a strange story, Poole,' said Utterson. 'But if Dr Jekyll was murdered, why does the murderer stay there? There is no good reason for that.'

'No, there's no good reason,' Poole agreed. 'But I must tell you more. All this week, the person or thing in that room has cried day and night for some sort of medicine. And he can't get what he wants. In the past Dr Jekyll sometimes wrote his orders on a piece of paper and threw it on the stairs. For a week we've had only orders and a closed door. Orders for meals, but usually orders for a chemical.

'I took these orders to every chemist in London. And every time I brought the chemical back, there was another paper. It told me to take the chemical back. It wasn't right. It told me to try another chemist. I don't know what the chemical is for, Mr Utterson. But I know that the person in that room wants it very badly.'

'Do you have any of those papers, Poole?' asked Mr Utterson.

'Yes sir,' said Poole. He put a hand in his pocket and took out a note, then he gave it to Utterson. 'The man at Maw and Company was very angry and he threw this one back at me. I kept it.'

Utterson read the note:

Maw and Company:
You have sent me a chemical which is useless to me. In the year 1875 I bought a large amount of this chemical from you. Now I must ask you to make a very careful search. If you have any of *this old* (good) chemical, please send it to me immediately. The cost does not matter. This is very important.

28

Then came the last sentence. The writer ended:

God help me! Please find me some of the old chemical.
Henry Jekyll

'It does seem to be Dr Jekyll's writing,' said Mr Utterson.

'Yes,' said Poole, 'but it isn't Dr Jekyll up there. I know because I've seen him!'

'You've seen him?' said the lawyer.

'Yes, sir,' said Poole.

'When?'

'I came suddenly into the workroom from the garden, and he was there in front of me,' said Poole. 'He probably came down secretly into the workroom to look for this chemical. His face was covered, and he was searching in the boxes in the workroom like a madman.'

'Did he see you?' asked the lawyer.

'Yes, sir,' replied Poole.

'What happened?' asked Utterson.

'When he saw me, he gave a cry. Then he ran up the stairs to the room above,' said Poole. 'This person's face was covered, but it wasn't the doctor.'

'His face was covered, you say,' said Utterson. 'Perhaps he is hurt. Perhaps he covers it because he does not want to shock his friends.'

'No, sir,' said Poole. 'Dr Jekyll is a tall, strong man. This man was small. And when I saw him I felt sick.'

Mr Utterson looked at the frightened servant. 'We must speak honestly, Poole,' he said. 'This person with the covered face – do you know who it was?'

'You mean, was it Mr Hyde? Yes, sir, I think it was,' said Poole. 'He gave you the feeling that he was all evil.'

'I know that feeling,' said the lawyer. 'Now listen, Poole. I will have to break down the door of the room above the workroom.'

'Oh, sir,' Poole cried, 'I'm very glad to hear you say that. I'll come with you. We'll do it together. There's an axe and a piece of metal in the workroom.'

'This will be dangerous,' said Utterson.

'I know that, sir,' said Poole.

◆

They sent two men-servants to watch the door into the narrow street.

'Poole and I are going to break into the room above the workroom,' Utterson told them. 'You must guard the door and stop anybody escaping. Take some big sticks to protect yourselves.'

Then Mr Utterson and Poole went to the door of the room. They listened. Somebody was walking up and down inside.

'Jekyll,' cried Utterson loudly, 'I must see you.'

The walking stopped, but there was no answer.

'If you don't open the door,' called the lawyer, 'we'll break it down. I must see you.'

'Utterson,' they heard from the other side of the door. 'Have pity on me!'

'That's not Jekyll's voice,' said Utterson. 'It's Hyde's! The door must come down.'

It was a very well-made door, and very strong. They had to use the axe many times before they could break the lock. They opened the door.

The two men looked into the room. It looked like other rooms, but there were cupboards full of chemicals and tables for scientific work. There was a good warm fire burning in the fireplace. A desk drawer was open and some papers were lying on the top. But on the floor, right in the middle of the room, was the body of a man.

The two men hurried across to it, and turned it over on to its back.

The face was Edward Hyde's.

The face was Edward Hyde's.

He was dressed in clothes that were too big for him. But the clothes were the right size for Dr Jekyll. There was a broken glass in his hand and a strong smell came from it. He was dead.

'I am afraid that we have arrived too late,' Mr Utterson said. 'Hyde has killed himself. Now we can only look for the body of Dr Jekyll.'

◆

They searched the house, but they could not find the body. The door into the narrow street was locked, and the broken key was on the floor inside the door.

'I don't understand this, Poole,' said Mr Utterson. 'Let's go back upstairs.'

They went back to the room and to the body of Mr Hyde. On one table there were small piles of some sort of white chemical on glass plates.

'That's the chemical which he sent me out for,' Poole said.

'For an experiment?' said Utterson.

There was a large envelope on the desk. The name 'Mr Utterson' was written on it in Dr Jekyll's handwriting. The lawyer opened it. Three things fell out.

The first thing was a new will. Like Dr Jekyll's first will, it spoke of his death or disappearance. But it was not Edward Hyde who now received everything. The lawyer was very surprised to read the name 'John Utterson.'

Utterson looked at Poole, then back at the papers, then at the body on the floor.

'I don't understand this,' he said. 'Hyde has been here all this time. He saw this new will, and he had no reason to like me. My name is on the paper in place of his. I feel sure that he was very angry about that. But he hasn't destroyed the will. It is very strange.'

He picked up the next paper. It was a short note in the doctor's handwriting, and the date was at the top.

'Poole!' he cried.

'What is it?' said Poole.

Mr Utterson was excited. 'Dr Jekyll was here and alive today!' he said. 'He is still alive, because no murderer could hide a body so quickly. Surely he has escaped! But why? How? And where did he go? There are a lot of questions here without answers. If we tell people about this death, perhaps we will make trouble for the doctor. Oh, we must be very careful, Poole!'

'Why don't you read the note, sir?' asked Poole.

'Because I'm afraid,' replied the lawyer. 'I hope that I have no reason to be afraid, but–'

'Please, read it, sir,' said Poole.

So Utterson looked at the note:

> My dear Utterson,
>
> When this is in your hands, my disappearance will be a fact. I don't know how it will happen. I do know that it will happen soon. So please go. Read the paper that Lanyon gave you. And then, if you want to know more, read my story.
>
> Your unhappy friend,
>
> Henry Jekyll

'Where is the third thing?' asked Utterson.

'Here, sir.' Poole picked up a thick envelope from the floor and gave it to the lawyer.

Utterson put it in his pocket. 'Let's say nothing about this yet,' he said.

'All right, sir,' said Poole.

'If the doctor has escaped, we can perhaps save his good name,' said Mr Utterson. 'It is ten o'clock now. I must go home and read these papers in a quiet place. But I will be back before midnight, and then we will send for the police.'

They went out, locking the door of the workroom behind them.

'Goodbye, Poole,' said Mr Utterson.

'Goodbye, sir,' said Poole. 'And thank you.'

Utterson walked home. There he read the two papers which explained the mystery.

Chapter 11   Dr Lanyon's Story

On the ninth of January, four days ago, I, Dr Hastie Lanyon, received a letter in the evening post. My name and address on the envelope were in the handwriting of my old school friend, Dr Henry Jekyll.

I was surprised by this because we did not often write. We met often for dinner and I could not think of anything important enough for a letter.

This was the letter:

9 December 1881

Dear Lanyon,

You are one of my oldest friends. If, one day, you ever say to me, 'Jekyll, my life, my good name, my mind are in danger,' I will do everything to help you.

Now, Lanyon, *my* life, *my* good name and *my* mind are all in great danger. If you don't help me tonight, I am finished.

I ask you to do this after you have read this letter. Drive straight to my house. Poole, my servant, is waiting for you. He will take you to the door of the room above my workroom. I want you to go in alone. Open the cupboard with the letter "E" on the left – break the lock if necessary. Pull out the fourth drawer from the top. Inside it there are some chemicals, a bottle, and a notebook. Please take the drawer to your house.

At midnight, please be alone in your office. A man will come. Give him the drawer. That is all that I ask

you to do. Five minutes after that, you will understand
how important this is to me. I do not believe that you
will fail me. I am sure that you will do this.

　　With all my thanks,

H.J.

I was sure that the doctor was mad. But until that was proved, I
had to complete his request. I got a taxi and went immediately to
Jekyll's house. The servant was waiting there for me; he, too, had a
letter with his orders from Dr Jekyll.

The cupboard with the letter "E" on it was not locked. I
took out the drawer, covered it with a cloth, and brought it back
to my house.

When I was home again, I looked at the things in the drawer.
They were what Jekyll described. But it soon became clear that
the chemicals were prepared by Jekyll and not by a chemist. I
opened one of the packets and found something white. It looked
like salt, but it wasn't. I next looked at a small bottle of blood-red
liquid. I opened it, and it smelled very strongly. I could not name
the smell, but it was very unpleasant.

There was very little in the notebook except dates. There was
sometimes a word or two after the date; 'Double' is an example,
and once, early in the list, 'Completely failed!!!' I could only
guess their meanings. How did these things help me to do
anything for the life, the good name or the mind of the doctor?
It looked like the work of a madman.

'And why couldn't Jekyll's messenger go to Jekyll's house and
get these things?' I thought. 'Why did I have to go for him?'

◆

I sent my servants to bed, and at midnight I was waiting alone in
my office with the drawer − and a gun.

There was a quiet knock at the door. I opened it. I found a
small man trying to stay in the dark shadows.

35

'Are you from Dr Jekyll?' I asked.

He made a noise that I understood as 'yes'. I told him to come in. He saw a policeman come into the square on the far side, and he fearfully hurried inside.

This worried me a little, and I kept my hand on the gun in my pocket. I took him into the bright light of the office, and there I studied my visitor. He was a stranger to me. He was small, as I have said, and ugly. And I noticed that I had a very strong feeling of dislike and sickness. His clothes were expensive and very well-made, but they were too big for him. Unusually, that did not amuse me.

He was worried and excited at the same time. 'Have you got it?' he cried. 'Have you got it?'

He put his hand on my arm to shake me. I pushed it off.

'You forget, sir,' I said, 'that we have not met in the usual way. Please sit down.'

'I am very sorry, Dr Lanyon,' he said. He sat down. 'You are quite right. Your friend Dr Henry Jekyll sent me here on an important piece of business. And I understand that a drawer . . .'

I pointed to the drawer. 'There it is, sir,' I said.

He jumped out of his seat, and almost ran to it. Then he stopped suddenly and put his hand over his heart. His face was white, and I was afraid for his life and his mind.

'You must be calm,' I said.

He gave me a terrible smile, picked up the drawer, and looked at the things in it. He saw that they were all there. Then he said to me, 'Do you have a glass?'

I gave him what he wanted. He put some of the liquid from the bottle into the glass. Then he put in some of the chemical and mixed the two together. The liquid seemed to get brighter, and began to smell even more strongly than before. My visitor watched it closely, then he put the glass down on the table.

He looked at me carefully. 'Now, will you be sensible?' he said. 'Can I take this glass away without any questions? Or must you have answers? Think carefully before you reply. I can leave now – or you can watch something terribly shocking.'

'I want to see the end of this,' I said.

'Lanyon,' he said. 'Do you remember your promise when you became a doctor of medicine? This is a secret. Remember your promise, and keep it a secret.'

He put the glass to his mouth and drank the liquid – all of it. I watched him. With a cry, he reached for the table and nearly fell down. His eyes opened wide and strange noises came from his mouth.

Then he began to change.

He seemed to get bigger. His face suddenly went black, and parts of it moved – *like liquid*.

I was frightened, and I jumped back against the wall, away from him. I put a hand to my mouth. 'Oh, God!' I heard myself crying, again and again.

There, in front of my eyes – pale and shaking, like a man back from death – *there was Henry Jekyll*!

I just cannot write down the things that he told me in the next hour. I saw what I saw. I heard what I heard. Now I ask myself, 'Do I believe it?' And I cannot answer that question.

I cannot sleep. A terrible fear is with me every hour of every day and night. I cannot think about the evil man, and the terrible things that he told me, without fear.

I know that I shall soon die. But I will die without understanding. I can only tell you one thing, Utterson. The evil person in my house that night was a man called Hyde. The murderer of Sir Danvers Carew. The man that every policeman in the country is looking for.

Hastie Lanyon

Then he began to change.

Chapter 12   Henry Jekyll's Story

I, Dr Henry Jekyll, was born in the year 1830. My family was rich. I studied to be a doctor. I liked the hard work. Other people soon had a good opinion of me, and I liked that too. I seemed to have a good future in front of me. Everything looked bright and good.

My worst problem was my love of fun. I enjoyed the wild night life too much. Many people have found that a love of fun helps them to enjoy life. I wanted to seem serious, and this did not help. So I was careful to hide this side of my life. In this way, my life became a lie. Even before I finished my studies, I already had a double life. My actions were not serious, but I did not want them to be a part of my working life.

The years passed, and I grew older and more sensible. But it was too late to change my double life. And then, through my scientific studies, I learned something important. I learned that man has two sides – a good side and an evil side. I knew that this was true of me. I was honest about it. As a doctor, I tried to learn more and to help sick and suffering people. The other part of me was also honest about its search. Slowly it became clear to me that man is not just one person. He is two people.

'Can I separate the two sides?' I asked myself. 'Can I make two people – one good, one bad – from a single person? If I can, life will be much easier. The bad person can live in his own bad way, without hurting the good person and people's opinion of him. And the good person's good name will be in no danger because of the other person's bad actions. It seems wrong that we have to live with both persons in the same body.'

At that time I was doing some scientific work. I found that some chemicals have a great power. They can change a person's body – they can change its shape, and make it bigger or smaller. I do not want to be too clear about the scientific part of this story.

My reason? Because, as my story will show, my experiments were not completed.

It was a long time before I decided to try the chemicals. There were too many things that could go wrong. I was afraid of dying. But finally I had to know! I had to have the answer!

My experiments showed me the liquid that was necessary. Then I bought from Maw and Company – the chemists – a lot of the special salt chemical that I needed to put into it. Late one night, I carefully put the salt chemical and liquid into a glass and mixed them together. I watched the liquid change colour. Then, nervously, I drank what was in the glass.

I felt terrible pain and a great sickness. But then, quite quickly, the pain went away and I began to feel better! I felt younger, lighter, happier, and free in my body. My mind felt free, too. But I knew immediately that I was more evil than every other man on earth. How did I know this? I do not know. But it was a wonderful feeling! Like the taste of the best wine!

I looked down at my body. I saw immediately that I was smaller than before. There was no mirror in my workroom then – I brought it in later. So that night I went quickly across the dark courtyard and into the house. It was after midnight. All my servants were asleep, so they did not see me.

I went quietly up to my bedroom and straight to my mirror. In it, for the first time, I saw the man that I decided to call Edward Hyde. He was much smaller and younger than Henry Jekyll. I can only believe that the evil side of me was not fully grown. It was not as strong as my good side. The worst part of me was not as old and tired as the good and honest part.

The ugly face in the mirror was an evil face, I knew that. But I felt no fear. I welcomed it, because it seemed very natural. The face looked more alive than my usual face.

Later I realized that people could not come near me without a feeling of great dislike. They hated me before I even spoke.

'This is probably because they have never met a man like Edward Hyde. He is a man who is all bad – all evil,' I told myself. 'Most people are good and bad.'

Now came the next part of my experiment. I returned to my workroom and prepared the chemical again – and drank it. Once again I suffered the terrible pains of change. But I soon had the face and body of Henry Jekyll.

That night my life changed for ever. The experiment was a success, and from that time I was two people. One was Edward Hyde – a man completely evil. The other man was dear old Henry Jekyll.

As time passed, I felt a greater and greater need to escape into the younger, more exciting body of Edward Hyde. And it was so easy. I only had to drink the liquid, and there I was! In my new life.

I prepared everything carefully. As Hyde, I took the house in Soho and employed a woman. She looked after it and asked no questions. As Jekyll, I described Mr Hyde and told my servants: 'Mr Hyde can use my house in the square when he wants to use it.' I visited the house two or three times as Mr Hyde so there were no mistakes. His visits became quite usual.

At times Henry Jekyll was shocked and frightened by the things that Edward Hyde did. But only Hyde did wrong. Jekyll was not worse than before the experiment. He often tried to correct the wrong things that were done by Hyde.

Then I made the will that you did not like. Why did I make it? Because I wanted to be able to change from Dr Jekyll to Edward Hyde without losing all my money.

I would not like to describe everything that I did as Edward Hyde but I will tell you about one accident. It happened one night. I knocked down a child, and this made another man very angry. I saw the man the other day – he is your friend. The child's family were very angry, too. For a time I was afraid that they wanted to kill me. But Edward Hyde calmed them. He brought them to the workroom door and gave them a cheque from Henry Jekyll.

But most of the time, everything seemed perfect. If I was in trouble as Hyde, I only had to escape into my workroom through the door in the narrow street. I only needed a minute to make and drink the liquid. Then Edward Hyde disappeared! In his place, sitting quietly at his desk, was good, honest Henry Jekyll!

Edward Hyde was an evil man. Slowly, his actions got worse and worse. Then, two months before the murder of Sir Danvers Carew, I – Henry Jekyll – went out one evening and returned late. When I woke up the next morning, I looked down at my hand. The skin on it was darker, and it was half-covered in thick hair!

It was the hand of Edward Hyde!

I looked at it for almost a minute before I jumped out of bed. I ran to the mirror and looked at my face. Yes! There it was! There was no mistake!

'I went to bed as Henry Jekyll, but I have woken up as Edward Hyde!' I thought. 'How could it happen? What went wrong? And what am I going to do?'

All my chemicals were in my workroom, but I had to get to them. It was late in the morning and my servants were already working in the house. But I had to go through the house and across the courtyard. Then I remembered!

'Of course!' I thought. 'The servants have seen Edward Hyde in the house before now!' And I laughed.

I dressed quickly and went downstairs. One of my servants saw me. He looked a little shocked when he saw Edward Hyde so early in the day. But he said nothing. I hurried across the courtyard as fast as I could. I went straight to my workroom and quickly mixed the liquid. Then I drank it.

Ten minutes later, Dr Jekyll returned to the house for his breakfast.

Chapter 13   The End of the Story

After this, I began to think more seriously about my two different lives. When I was Henry Jekyll, I knew very well about Mr Hyde's activities.

And I began to see a new danger.

'Hyde is becoming too evil, too strong,' I thought. 'Perhaps a time will come soon when I will not be able to change back to Dr Henry Jekyll. Hyde will have too much power. I shall be with him for the rest of my life.'

I knew that it was a real danger. Sometimes I had to make the liquid two or three times stronger than usual before I could change back from Hyde to Dr Jekyll.

I had to choose between these two. Jekyll or Hyde? Jekyll did not have the excitement, the almost pleasant dangers of Hyde's life. But Hyde did not work as a doctor. He was hated and he had no friends.

I decided not to bring Hyde back again. I preferred the old (and perhaps boring) doctor with his friends, I decided. So I said goodbye to Hyde. I missed feeling younger. I missed the excitement of Hyde's life. But for two months I did not bring him back.

Then, in an hour of weakness, I went to my workroom and made the terrible liquid – and brought him back again.

I was frightened by what happened next. Hyde was a prisoner for two months, so now he was like a wild animal! I could feel the new power of his evil ways. He wanted to shout and scream and hurt somebody.

Then I met the unlucky Sir Danvers Carew in the street. He asked me a simple question, and I enjoyed hitting him again and again. I only stopped when I was tired. I looked down at the broken body of the old man and, suddenly, I felt fear. Hyde was in danger! Hyde had to get away!

I ran through the dark shadows of the streets to my house in

Soho. I was shaking with fear and excitement. When I got to the house, I destroyed all my papers. Then I went out into the streets again and hurried to my workroom. There I felt safe.

I sang a song as I mixed the chemical and the liquid. I drank it and thought of the dead man – and laughed and laughed.

After the terrible pain of change ended, I (as Henry Jekyll) fell down on to my knees, because I was that good man again. I covered my face. I wanted to scream loudly when I thought of the terrible murder of that poor old man. Tears poured from my eyes. I asked God to forgive me.

◆

Next day, the newspapers were full of the story of the murder of Sir Danvers Carew. I read all of them. I learned for the first time that someone watched the murder from a window! And now the police had the name of the murderer – Edward Hyde!

The Carew murder made my future clear. It was impossible to bring Hyde back because the world was looking for him. The world was waiting to take the life of a murderer.

'I will never bring him back again!' I told myself. I locked the door from the workroom to the street and broke the key. 'I have finished with evil,' I promised myself. 'I will work harder. I will help weak, ill and suffering people.'

You know that I tried to do this during the last months of last year. I never dreamed of bringing the terrible Edward Hyde back again.

◆

On a fine, clear January day when there was not one cloud in the sky, I was sitting in the sun in Regent's Park. I was resting after a hard morning's work. The birds were singing and my mind was not busy. Perhaps I was sleepily remembering happier days when I was young.

Suddenly I had feelings of pain, sickness and shock. When the pain left me, I looked down. My clothes were hanging over the smaller body and legs of – Edward Hyde!

I could not believe it! A minute before, I was safe, rich, and loved. The good, honest Dr Jekyll. Now, suddenly, I was the man that everybody was looking for. A man without a home. A murderer.

I had to change back again – and quickly, before somebody saw me. But how could I get the chemicals that I needed? They were in my workroom, and the street door to the workroom was locked. I could not go into the house from the square. Everyone was looking for Mr Hyde – my servants too.

'What can I do?' I thought.

Hyde's mind was quicker than Jekyll's. He thought of Lanyon.

'How can I reach him?' I thought. 'And how can I, Hyde, ask him to steal things from his friend, Dr Jekyll?'

Then I remembered something, and I laughed,

'I can still write a letter in my handwriting,' I thought. And I knew immediately what I had to do.

I walked out of the park and stopped a passing taxi, then drove to Portland Street. The driver looked at the clothes that did not fit me. He was clearly amused, but he said nothing.

In Portland Street I went to a cheap hotel and asked for a private room. The man at the hotel desk looked at my clothes and smiled. But the look on my face quickly took the smile from his mouth. I asked for some paper, and he gave it to me. Then I went to the room. There I sat at a table and wrote two letters, one to Lanyon and one to Poole. Then I paid a servant at the hotel and he took them.

The rest of the day was a time of great fear. Most of the time I sat alone in the hotel room. A waiter brought my dinner to me, then I sat by the fire. When it was dark, I left the hotel. I walked through the empty streets of the city until midnight. I walked quickly and stayed in the shadows. Once a woman spoke to me, but I hit her across the face and she ran away.

I changed back to myself – to Dr Jekyll – at Lanyon's house. He was shocked, and the fear on my old friend's face hurt me. He was angry with me, of course. But the memory of those terrible hours as Hyde frightened me most. I was terribly afraid. Not afraid of a murderer's death, but afraid of being Hyde.

I listened to Lanyon's angry words, but I seemed to be in a dream. And I seemed to walk home and go to my bed in that same dream.

I slept well at home. In the morning I felt weak but calm. I hated the evil man who slept inside me. But I was at home in my own house again, near the chemicals that I needed.

After breakfast, I walked across the courtyard to my workroom. I was enjoying the cold but clear air. Then suddenly I began to change into Hyde again. I realized immediately what was happening. I had enough time to reach my room over the workroom. Then I was filled with the power of Hyde's evil.

I worked quickly. But I had to take double the usual amount of the liquid before I was Jekyll again.

Six hours after that, the pain and the change returned, and again I had to take the liquid.

From that day, only the chemical kept Hyde away. At all hours of the day and night I felt pain and suffered the change. When I slept, I woke up as Hyde. Even if I fell half-asleep for a minute in my chair, the same thing happened.

I was afraid to sleep. But when I stayed awake, the change still came. When the power of the chemical became weak, I became Hyde. Without sleep, and with the terrible fear, my health began to leave me.

And as Jekyll got weaker, Hyde grew stronger.

Now a last terrible thing has happened. I sent Poole for more chemicals when the chemicals from Maw and Company were nearly finished. I mixed them with the liquid, but they were not strong enough. The colour of the liquid was different. I drank it, but nothing happened.

Poole will tell you that he searched London for more chemicals. I believe now that there was something in those first chemicals. It was not there in the other chemicals. That unknown something gave the chemical its power.

About a week has passed. I am using the last of the old chemicals so I can write this to you. This is the last time that Henry Jekyll will have his own mind. He will not see his face (now terribly changed and old) in the mirror again. And I must bring my story to an end quickly. If the change comes now, Hyde will destroy this letter. But if I have already finished it, he will be too busy. He has to think of a way to escape the death of a murderer.

Will Hyde hang as a murderer? Or will he be brave? Will he kill himself and escape that death? I do not know. This is my real hour of death. The future will happen to another person. Here, then, I am putting my pen down and I am ending the life of the unhappy Henry Jekyll.

ACTIVITIES

Chapters 1–3

Before you read

1 Look at the Word List at the back of this book and check the meanings of new words. Then discuss these questions.

    a Think of three examples of evil actions. What makes them evil?

    b Are there experiments that, in your opinion, scientists mustn't do? If there are, what are they? Why are they wrong?

    c How can you know that someone is mad? What signs do you look for?

    d Why do wills often make problems in families? Do you know of any examples?

2 Read the Introduction to the book. Who:

    a is a good, honest man?

    b has power over him?

    c does dangerous experiments?

    d is killed?

    e is the murderer?

While you read

3 Are these sentences right (✓) or wrong (✗)?

    a Mr Utterson is a serious man. .....

    b Mr Enfield and Mr Utterson are friends. .....

    c Mr Enfield tells a story about a morning many years ago. .....

    d A man stepped on a child. .....

    e Then the man ran away. .....

    f Another man signed a cheque for the girl. .....

After you read

4 Discuss what you know about:

    a Mr Utterson

    b Mr Hyde

    c the man who signed the cheque

5 Work with another student. Have this conversation.

Student A: You are Mr Enfield. Tell your friend the story about Mr Hyde and the child.

Student B: You are Mr Utterson. Ask questions. Then tell your friend what you think about the story.

Chapters 4–5

Before you read

6 In Chapter 4, Mr Utterson looks at someone's will. Discuss these questions. What do you think?

a Who wrote the will?

b What does it say?

c Why does Mr Utterson not like it?

While you read

7 Finish the sentences. Write one word in each sentence.

a Mr Utterson takes the will from his ....

b Before Mr Enfield's story, Mr Utterson thought that Dr Jekyll was ....

c Now he thinks that Dr Jekyll is ....

d Dr Lanyon .... with some of Dr Jekyll's ideas.

e Mr Utterson thinks that Mr Hyde has .... over Dr Jekyll.

f When Mr Utterson first sees Mr Hyde, he feels great .... for him.

g Mr Hyde has a .... to the door of Dr Jekyll's courtyard.

h When Dr Jekyll is out, his servants take .... from Mr Hyde.

i Dr Jekyll says that he is .... in Mr Hyde.

j When Dr Jekyll dies, he wants Mr Utterson to .... Mr Hyde.

After you read

8 Discuss these questions.

    a What does Dr Jekyll's will say?

    b Why does Mr Utterson dislike the will?

    c Why does he dislike Mr Hyde?

    d How does Dr Jekyll show that he trusts Mr Hyde?

Chapters 6–7

Before you read

9 Which of these words describe Dr Jekyll? Which describe Mr Hyde?

ugly famous fine honest unpleasant friendly evil cold

10 Dr Jekyll says, 'When I want to, I can be free of Hyde.' What do you think he means?

While you read

11 Circle the right words to complete each sentence.

    a The crime happens ....

    some days later   a month later   a year later

    b Mr Hyde attacks ....

    a girl   a policeman   an old man

    c In the dead person's pocket there is a letter for ....

    Sir Danvers Carew   Mr Hyde   Mr Utterson

    d The broken stick belongs to ....

    Sir Danvers Carew   Dr Jekyll   Mr Utterson

    e The police find the other part of the stick in ....

    Mr Hyde's house   the street   Dr Jekyll's house

    f Dr Jekyll says that he ....

    is hiding Mr Hyde   hasn't seen Mr Hyde

    won't see Mr Hyde again

    g The letter from Mr Hyde was written by ....

    Dr Jekyll   Mr Hyde   Guest

12 Describe each of the pictures in these chapters. What can you see? What has happened? What is going to happen next?

Chapters 8–9

Before you read

13 The last sentence of Chapter 7 is: 'And the blood ran cold through his body.' Discuss what this means. How does Mr Utterson feel? Why? What will he do next?

While you read

14 What happens first? Put these sentences in the right order, from 1–7.

    a Dr Lanyon dies.   .....

    b Mr Utterson visits Dr Lanyon.   .....

    c Dr Jekyll refuses to see any visitors.   .....

    d Mr Hyde disappears.   .....

    e Dr Jekyll asks Mr Utterson to leave him alone.   .....

    f Dr Jekyll's servants are worried about him.   .....

    g Mr Utterson received a letter from Dr Lanyon.   .....

15 Who is speaking? Who or what are they talking about?

    a 'I had the same feelings of fear and hate that you described.'

    b 'God forgive us!'

After you read

16 Discuss these questions.

    a Why is Mr Utterson shocked by the letter from Dr Jekyll and the envelope from Dr Lanyon?

    b What is happening to Dr Jekyll?

17 Work with another student. Have this conversation.

    Student A: You are Mr Utterson. Your friend, Dr Lanyon, looks very ill – and afraid. Ask him questions.

    Student B: You are Dr Lanyon. Answer Mr Utterson's questions. You are happy to talk about your illness. But you don't want to talk about Dr Jekyll.

Chapters 10–11

18 Dr Lanyon saw something that gave him a terrible shock. What do you think it was? Discuss possible reasons for his shock.

19 At the beginning of Chapter 10, Poole arrives at Mr Utterson's house. What do you think he is going to tell Mr Utterson? What will Mr Utterson do?

While you read

20 Complete each sentence with a word on the right.

a	Dr Jekyll's servants are all . . .	axe.
b	The person in the room above the workroom sounds . . .	chemical.
		afraid.
c	That person has asked repeatedly for a . . .	envelope.
d	The note to the chemist is in Dr Jekyll's . . .	evil.
e	Poole saw a small man with a covered . . .	body.
f	Poole felt that the man was . . .	angry.
g	Mr Utterson and Poole break down the door with an . . .	handwriting.
		will.
h	On the floor of the room is Mr Hyde's . . .	face.
i	Mr Utterson and Poole find Dr Jekyll's new . . .	
j	They also find a note and an . . .	

21 What did Dr Jekyll tell Dr Lanyon to do? Which is the right word?

    a Open a cupboard with the letter *E / G* on it.

    b Open the *fourth / top* drawer.

    c Take the *note / drawer* to the doctor's house.

    d *Send / Give* the drawer to a man.

22 Answer these questions. Write one or two words.

    a Who came for the drawer? ....

    b Who sent him? ....

    c What did he mix with liquid from the bottle? ....

    d Who was he after he drank the liquid? ....

23 Discuss these questions.

    a Describe what happened to Mr Hyde as he changed into Dr Jekyll. How did Dr Lanyon feel? What did he realise as he watched?

    b Why can't Mr Utterson and Poole find Dr Jekyll's body?

Chapters 12–13

Before you read

24 Chapter 12 is Dr Jekyll's story. What do you think it will say?

While you read

25 Answer the questions. Write Yes or No.

    a Did Dr Jekyll enjoy his studies? ....

    b Did he also have fun as a student? ....

    c Did he want to be completely serious? ....

    d Did he use chemicals to change his body? ....

    e Did Edward Hyde look like Dr Jekyll? ....

    f Was Dr Jekyll ever shocked by Hyde? ....

    g Did the chemicals continue to work well? ....

    h Was Dr Jekyll happy about the murder? ....

    i Did Dr Jekyll decide to stop changing into Hyde? ....

    j Did Dr Lanyon understand Dr Jekyll's actions? ....

After you read

26 Imagine that you are one of the people below. Talk to the class.

    a You are Dr Lanyon. Dr Jekyll has just left your house. What happened while he was there? How do you feel now?

    b You are Mr Utterson. You have just read Dr Jekyll's story. What have you learnt? How do you feel about your friend now?

    c You are Poole. You have just realised that your employer is dead. How do you feel about him now?

    d You are the police officer who is looking for the murderer of Mr Danvers Carew. You have just heard about Mr Hyde's death. How do you feel about that?

Writing

27 You are a newspaper reporter. Write the story of Mr Hyde and the child for your newspaper.

28 You are the person who saw the murder of Sir Danvers Carew. Write a report for the police about what you saw.

29 You are Mr Hyde. Write about the murder of Sir Danvers Carew. What did you do? Why? How did you feel?

30 You are Poole. Dr Jekyll has locked himself in his room again and the servants are afraid. Write a note to Mr Utterson explaining why. Ask for his help.

31 You are Dr Lanyon. Write a letter to a scientific magazine about Dr Jekyll's experiments. Tell the scientists what happened.

32 You are Mr Utterson. Write a notice of Dr Jekyll's death for a newspaper. Write about the side of him that his friends and patients will miss.

33 Describe a person who you know well. Describe their good side and their bad side. Give examples of their actions to show these two sides.

34 Imagine that a drink will change you into a different person. What kind of person would you like to be?

35 Write about one area of science where successful experiments are good for everybody. Are there experiments that in your opinion scientists should never try to do? If there are, give two examples.

36 Did you enjoy the story of *Dr Jekyll and Mr Hyde*? Why (not)? Would you like to see a film of the story? Write your opinions.

WORD LIST

axe (n) a tool for cutting wood

chemical (n) something that chemists use in scientific tests

clerk (n) someone who works with papers in an office

client (n) someone who pays for the help of a professional person

courtyard (n) an open place with walls or buildings around it

drawer (n) a part of a piece of furniture. You open it by pulling it out.

evil (n/adj) the opposite of good; very bad

experiment (n) a scientific test

God (n) the one who made the Earth and everything on it

inspector (n) an important police officer

lawyer (n) a professional who has studied the law

liquid (n) something, like water, that you can pour

mad (adj) ill in the head, crazy

power (n) the ability to make decisions about other people's lives

safe (n) a strong box for money and important papers

separate (v) to put into two or more parts

servant (n) someone who works in another person's house

shock (n/v) a terrible surprise

trust (v) to believe that someone is honest. They will not lie to you or hurt you.

will (n) an important written paper. In it you leave your money by law to named people on your death.